The Country Kitchen

VEGETABLES

Anne Chapman

The Country Kitchen

VEGETABLES

Anne Chapman

HARLAXTON
PUBLISHING

Front and back jacket: Green olives, tomatoes, gramma squash squash pie (p. 40), carrots, peas and prosciutto (p. 11), asparagus, Florentine eggplant, Chinese winter melon, broccoli, cauliflower, honey-glazed carrots and parsnips (p. 9), fresh garden salad, (p. 29) pumpkin, various colored sweet peppers, red Spanish onions, 2 large gramma squash, butternut pumpkins, corn.

Front and back endpapers: An old-fashioned country kitchen with the preparation for a spicey fruit cake in the foreground. The wood burning stove is wonderful for long, slow cooking.

Page 2: Prosciutto cooked with green peas not only provides a new taste sensation but looks colorful on the table as well. Almost a meal in itself.

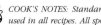 *COOK'S NOTES: Standard spoon measurements are used in all recipes. All spoon measurements are level.*

All ovens should be preheated to the specified temperature. Fresh herbs are used unless otherwise stated. If they are unavailable, use half the quantity of dried herbs. Use freshly ground black pepper whenever pepper is used; add salt and pepper to taste. Use all purpose flour unless otherwise stated. Extra virgin olive oil is used whenever oil is mentioned unless otherwise stated.

Published by Harlaxton Publishing Ltd
2 Avenue Road, Grantham, Lincolnshire, NG31 6TA, United Kingdom.
A Member of the Weldon International Group of Companies.

First published in 1992.
Reprinted in 1993.

© Copyright Harlaxton Publishing Ltd
© Copyright design Harlaxton Publishing Ltd

Publishing Manager: Robin Burgess
Project Coordinator: Barbara Beckett
Designer: Barbara Beckett
Illustrator: Amanda McPaul
Photographer: Ray Jarratt
Editor in United Kingdom: Alison Leach
Typeset in United Kingdom: Seller's, Grantham
Produced in Singapore by Imago

British Library Cataloguing-in-Publication data.
A catalogue record for this book is available from the British Library.
Title: Country Kitchen Series: Vegetables
ISBN:1 85837 008 6

CONTENTS

INTRODUCTION

THERE are many wonderful and delicious ways to present vegetables, not only as an accompaniment to the main meal but as a principal component of it. This is especially so in an increasingly health-conscious society. Vegetables, particularly those you can pick yourself retain all their nutrients, fiber and freshness-qualities which are essential for a healthy diet.

If you are going to store vegetables, it is important to do so correctly. Salad vegetables, for example, should be kept in the crisper drawer of the refrigerator, which will keep them fresh for up to a week. Other vegetables should be stored in a cool, airy place.

Remember, even at the end of their short shelf-life, vegetables may be used in your stock preparations, rather than thrown away. Even when you do throw them out, make sure, if possible, they go into the compost and

A simple gelatin mold of your favorite vegetables makes a nutritious lunch on a hot day. Carrots, asparagus and scallions decorated with Italian parsley leaves form the basis of this mold.

are recycled through your garden

Vegetables that are not going to be eaten fresh in salads need to be prepared and cooked properly. There are many ways of doing so, which will be encountered as you work your way through the recipes in this book. One of the most common is the purée method, which transforms the vegetables into a form that can be easily stored in the freezer. Most vegetables can be treated in this way and reconstituted at a later date to be eaten as an accompaniment to the main meal or in soups. Stewed or braised vegetables, such as celery, or cabbage, keep for several days in the refrigerator and have a wonderful flavor, even an enhanced one, when returned to room temperature or reheated slowly. Most vegetables, however, like snap beans, brussel sprouts or cabbage, require only short cooking periods to preserve their crispness and crunchiness.

One of the interesting things about vegetables is their versatility as a dessert, and for tarts, cakes and breads. Some attention has been given to this in the chapter *'Preserves and Sweets'*.

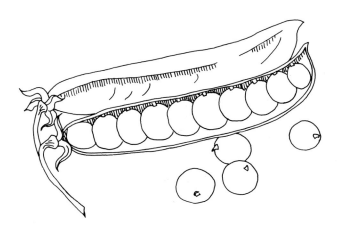

HOT VEGETABLE DISHES

Braised Cabbage in Wine

It is the wine that flavors this cabbage dish, so don't be a miser and use your second best.

2	tablespoons oil
1	large onion, thinly sliced
1	teaspoon rosemary
1	medium head of cabbage, coarsely shredded
1	tablespoon thick tomato purée (p. 45)
1	cup dry white wine
	Salt and pepper

Heat the oil in a large saucepan, add the onion and rosemary and sauté over a medium heat until the onion becomes translucent. Add the cabbage, cover the pot and cook for 5 minutes until it begins to wilt, stirring from time to time to prevent sticking. Add the rest of the ingredients, replace the cover and cook slowly over a low heat for about 20 minutes until the cabbage is tender. Serves 6-8.

Roast Carrots & Parsnips with Honey

A most beautiful side dish for any meat course. If your herb garden is bristling with rosemary or thyme flowers–sprinkle them before serving.

4	parsnips, peeled
4	carrots, peeled
2	tablespoons clear honey
1	tablespoon sunflower oil
4	tablespoons rosemary or thyme flowers (optional)

Buttered Snap Beans

For best results, choose very small crisp beans. It is not always easy to find them in the stores, so why not try to grow your own.

1	pound snap beans
	Salt
1	tablespoon butter
2	tablespoons chopped parsley

Wash the beans, top and tail them and place them in a saucepan. Season with salt and cover with boiling water. Boil for no more than 8 minutes, until the beans are just tender. Do not overcook, or they will become too soft and lose color. Better control can be maintained if you use a microwave. Drain the beans and rinse with cold or iced water to stop the beans cooking any further. If you slightly undercook the beans, this step in the preparation can be done well ahead. Just before serving, melt the butter in a saucepan and toss the beans in it until well coated and hot. Sprinkle with the parsley and serve. Serves 4.

Coat the carrots and parsnips with the honey and oil mixture. Arrange them in a baking dish and roast in a preheated oven at 375°F for about an hour, basting frequently. When the vegetables are a golden-brown and cooked through, transfer to a serving dish, sprinkle with herb flowers and serve immediately. This quantity is obviously for 4 people. If you have large vegetables, split them down the center; this will increase the portions.

Roast carrots and parsnips with honey glaze and rosemary flowers is a dish fit to grace any table.

Fava Beans with Cream & Bacon

2	pounds fava beans
1	cup chicken stock (p. 42)
1	teaspoon superfine sugar
	A bouquet garni
1	egg yolk
1/2	cup light cream
	Salt and pepper
1/4	cup finely shredded cooked bacon

Cook the beans in the stock with sugar and herbs until the beans are just tender. Remove the bouquet garni and discard. Beat the egg yolk with the cream and stir carefully into the beans. Heat gently and season with salt and pepper. Transfer to a warm serving dish and sprinkle with crispy bacon. Serves 4-6.

Stir-Fried Broccoli

When it comes down to simple stir-fry dishes, nationalities are only distinguished by the oil they use:for example olive for Italian style, peanut for Chinese cuisine.

1	pound broccoli
3	tablespoons olive or peanut oil
3	garlic cloves, coarsely chopped
1/4	teaspoon superfine sugar (Chinese style)

Break up the broccoli into florets and remove excess stem. In a steamer, cook the broccoli until just tender. In a separate pan, heat the oil and fry the garlic; do not burn it. Add sugar at this stage if you are cooking Chinese style. Stir broccoli into the pan and turn until it is hot and coated with the oil and garlic. Serves 4.

The unusual combination of Jerusalem artichoke and garlic adds a new dimension to the main meal. A very tasty vegetable accompaniment.

Spiced Carrots

Carrots originally came from the Middle East, where they are treated in a very spicey and sweet fashion.

2	tablespoons oil
3	garlic cloves, finely chopped
1	tablespoon crushed cumin seeds
2	small dried chilies, chopped (optional)
2	pounds carrots, cut into strips lengthwise
1/2	cup water
1/4	teaspoon superfine sugar
1	tablespoon lemon juice
	Salt

In a large pan, heat the oil and sauté the garlic over a low heat for 1 minute. Add the cumin and chilies and the carrots and toss for several minutes to glaze the vegetables. Add the water, sugar and lemon juice and season with salt to taste. Cover the pan and cook over a medium heat until the carrots are just tender and the liquid absorbed. Serves 6.

COOK'S NOTES: Do not add salt to beans when cooking them, as it only toughens them and prolongs the cooking time.

Chayotes with Red Chilies

The chayote (known as choko, christophene or custard pear in some regions) It will stay fresh in the refrigerator for at least a month; it can be boiled, sautéed or steamed, used in pickles and chutneys or even sweetened as a dessert.

3	small chayotes
6	red chilies
4	tablespoons refined peanut oil
1/2	teaspoon salt
4	tablespoons water
1	teaspoon sherry

Cut the chayotes open, get rid of the seed and other white tissue and remove the outside skin, then wash and slice them. Cut the chilies into small pieces and stir-fry in the oil in a pan. Add the chayote slices to the pan and sprinkle with salt. Pour the water in while stir-frying, cover and simmer for no more than 2 minutes. Remove the cover, drip the sherry over and serve immediately. Serves 4.

Jerusalem Artichokes

4	garlic cloves, finely sliced
2	tablespoons butter or oil
1	pound Jerusalem artichokes
	Water or vegetable stock

Sauté the garlic in butter or oil until golden. Meanwhile, scrub the Jerusalem artichokes well under cold water, then cut horizontally into 1/4-inch slices. Add the artichokes to the pan, cover and simmer over low heat until tender yet crisp, checking after a few minutes to see if more liquid is required. If so, add a small amount of water or vegetable stock. Turn out onto a warm serving plate. Serves 4.

Snow Peas with Carrots & Mint

A wonderful combination of taste and color. You can use lemon thyme, basil, chives or marjoram instead of mint.

1	pound carrots, peeled
2	tablespoons butter
	Salt
1	cup water
1	pound snow peas, stem ends and strings removed
1/4	cup chopped mint

Cut the carrots into strips about 1/4-inch wide and 2-inches long. In a pan, combine the carrots with half the butter and the salt and water. Cover the pan and simmer for about 6 minutes. Place the snow peas in a pot of boiling, salted water and cook for no more than 2 minutes. Drain. Remove the lid from the carrots and shake the pan over high heat to reduce the liquid to a glaze. Add the peas and the remaining tablespoon of butter and heat through. Serve immediately, sprinkled with mint. Serves 6.

Peas & Prosciutto

2	ounces prosciutto
2	tablespoons butter or margarine
2	pounds peas, freshly shelled
12	scallions, peeled and sliced
1	teaspoon superfine sugar
	Salt and pepper
1/2	cup chicken stock (p. 42)
	Sprigs of mint

Cut prosciutto into thin strips and add to the melted butter in a large pan. Stir in the peas and then the remaining ingredients except for the mint. bring to a boil, cover the pan and simmer over a low heat. Cook gently for no more than 15 minutes. Transfer to a warm serving dish and decorate with sprigs of mint. Serves 4.

Lemon Potatoes

2	pounds small new potatoes
	Peel of half a lemon
4	tablespoons butter
1/2	cup lemon juice
	Salt and pepper
2	tablespoons chopped mint

Wash and scrub the potatoes and place in a pot, covering them with lightly salted water. Add the lemon peel. Bring to a boil and cook until tender. Drain. In a large skillet, heat the butter and lemon juice and toss the potatoes in the mixture for about 5 minutes. Serve sprinkled with salt and pepper. Garnish with the mint (or any other herb). Serves 6.

Potatoes & Herbs

I sometimes give a lift to baked potatoes with herbs in the following manner.

6	white potatoes of uniform size
1/2	cup flour
	Salt and pepper
1	teaspoon thyme leaves
1	teaspoon chopped marjoram
1	teaspoon chopped chervil or parsley
3	tablespoons butter
3	small garlic cloves, unpeeled
1	bay leaf

Wash and peel the potato   nd leave whole. Season the flour with salt and pepper and the herbs; roll the potatoes in it until completely covered. Arrange the potatoes in a buttered casserole dish and dot with the butter. Add the garlic and bay leaf to the dish, cover with foil and bake in a preheated oven at 400°F for 45 minutes or until the potatoes are tender. Serves 6.

Potatoes & Onions Indian-Style

1/2	cup vegetable oil
1	teaspoon black mustard seeds
2	tablespoons finely chopped ginger root
1	green chili, seeded and finely chopped
1	tablespoon ground coriander
1	teaspoon turmeric
1/2	teaspoon paprika
4	cups potatoes, boiled and cubed
3	cups onions chopped
1	quart water
1	teaspoon salt
1	tablespoon lemon juice
4	tablespoons chopped cilantro leaves

Heat the oil over a high heat in a wok or deep pan. When the oil is hot, add the mustard seeds and cover immediately. Cook for 1 or 2 minutes until the seeds 'pop'. Reduce the heat slightly and add the ginger and chili and cook for 2 minutes more.

Add the ground coriander, turmeric and paprika and stir into the ginger and chili mixture. Add the potatoes and onions and sauté for 10 minutes, stirring all the time. Add the water and sprinkle with the salt. Cover the pan once more and simmer the vegetables for about 15 minutes. Stir in the lemon juice and turn out into a warm serving bowl. Sprinkle with chopped cilantro leaves. Serves 8.

COOK'S NOTES: Cooking time for carrots varies enormously depending on the season. Old carrots take a lot longer to cook than young ones.

The floury taste of new potatoes, cooked in their skins to retain their full nutritional value, blends wonderfully with the lemon dressing and mint.

Radishes glazed with orange and butter make a delicious and colorful combination of tastes.

Radishes with Orange Glaze

Radishes are mostly used as a salad vegetable. Try this interesting departure as a hot accompaniment to beef roast.

1	*pound radishes*
1	*orange*
1	*tablespoon sweet butter*
1/8	*teaspoon salt*
	Pepper

Trim the radishes of their stem and root ends and wash well. Place the radishes in a steamer, cover and cook for about 15 minutes-steaming rather than boiling is the best cooking process to use here. The radishes should be tender but still slightly firm.

Meanwhile, pare thin strips of peel from the orange and chop it very finely, to make 1 tablespoon. Squeeze the juice from the orange and set it aside.

In a large skillet, melt the butter over a medium heat and add orange juice. Simmer for 3 minutes until the mixture becomes syrupy in texture. Transfer the radishes to the skillet, season with salt and pepper and sauté the vegetables until evenly coated with the orange glaze, about 2 minutes. Stir in the orange peel and serve immediately. Serves 6.

SOUPS

Mixed Vegetable Soup with Leeks

A hearty rich vegetable soup for cold nights.

2	tablespoons butter
1	chopped Spanish (red) onion
1	pound pumpkin, cubed
1	cup potatoes, cubed
1/2	cup fava beans, shelled
2	cups milk
	Salt
1/8	teaspoon cayenne
1	small leek, sliced
2	cups chicken stock, heated (p. 42)
1/2	cup boiled rice
1/2	cup light cream
2	tablespoons chopped parsley

In a large saucepan melt half the butter and sauté the onions until tender. Add the pumpkin, potatoes, beans and milk. bring to a boil, then lower heat and simmer for 45 minutes. Stir occasionally so that the vegetables do not stick to the bottom of the pan. Transfer the mixture to a food processor in batches and blend. Return the purée to a clean saucepan and season with salt and cayenne.

In a small skillet, melt the remaining butter and sauté the leek. Add to the vegetable purée along with the chicken stock and bring slowly to a boil. Simmer for 10 minutes, then stir in the boiled rice, cream and chopped parsley.
Serves 6-8.

Celeriac Soup

Celeriac is not a handsome vegetable to look at. It is a celery grown for its root and is used in both salads and soups.

2	tablespoons butter
2	medium onions, sliced
2	large celeriac roots, about 2 pounds trimmed weight
1	pound potatoes, diced
1	teaspoon salt
1/2	teaspoon celery seeds
3	cups water
2	cups milk
	White pepper

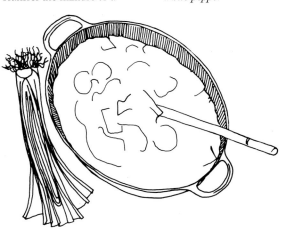

In a large casserole dish, heat the butter over a low heat. Add the onions; cover and cook until golden. They should take about 10 minutes. Stir occasionally.

Wash and peel the celeriac and cut into thick slices. Add to the onions along with the potatoes, salt and celery seeds. Stir so that all are coated with the butter. Add the water and milk, cover the casserole and simmer the vegetables until tender–about 30 minutes.

Transfer the mixture in batches to a food processor and process for only a few seconds. The soup should retain its chunky texture. Return the soup to the casserole dish, season with white pepper and dilute with more milk if you find the consistency a little too thick for your taste. Reheat gently. Serves 4.

Eggplant & Yogurt Soup

The distinctive taste of eggplants is synonymous with Greek cooking. This delicious soup will brighten any summer lunch.

6	medium-size eggplant
1/4	cup oil
3	green sweet peppers, skinned, seeded and chopped
1	quart natural yogurt
1	teaspoon salt
1/2	teaspoon pepper
1/8	teaspoon cayenne
2	garlic cloves, crushed
1	tablespoon chopped mint leaves

Remove the dark skin from the eggplants, slice in half lengthwise and salt the cut surfaces. Set aside to sweat, cut side up, for 30 minutes. Wipe dry and squeeze gently to remove bitter juices. Warm the oil in a large skillet and sauté the eggplants and sweet peppers, but do not brown. When tender, transfer to a food processor and purée. Mix thoroughly with yogurt and add the rest of the ingredients. This soup should be served ice-cold. Serves 4-6.

Chilled Gazpacho

3	pounds tomatoes
3	shallots
2	English cucumbers
1/4	cup oil
1/4	cup lemon juice
	Salt and pepper
	Tabasco sauce
1	cup Spanish (red) onion, chopped
2	green sweet peppers
	Seasoned croûtons

Blanch the tomatoes in hot water for 5 minutes. Peel and core them and cut into chunky pieces. In a food processor fitted with a metal blade, purée the tomatoes in batches of about 2 cups. Peel the shallots and add to the last batch of tomatoes. Turn out the mixture into a large bowl, after passing it through a strainer to remove the seeds.

Peel one cucumber, halve it lengthways and scoop out any large seeds. Cut into small pieces

A bowl of thick celeriac soup can be a meal in itself. The flavor of celery blended with potatoes and onion is a winning combination.

and blend in the food processor, adding the oil and lemon juice throughout the blending process. Add the cucumber mixture to the tomato purée, season with salt and pepper and add a few drops of Tabasco sauce. Mix well, cover and refrigerate for several hours.

Peel and chop the onion and set aside, covered, in the refrigerator. Peel the second cucumber, halve it and remove the seeds. Dice it and refrigerate. Char the sweet peppers in the oven or under the broiler and discard the skin, stem, ribs and seeds. Chop into small pieces and refrigerate.

Before serving, mix all the prepared vegetables together. Add a few ice cubes to the soup and serve in individual bowls. Garnish with croûtons. Serves 8.

 COOK'S NOTES: Nothing compares with fresh asparagus, which, when at its best, grows in sandy soil. Some sand always clings to the top as it pushes through the earth, so wash it well to eliminate all traces of sand.

On a hot summer's evening, with a glass of chilled white wine, Spanish gazpacho soup is one of the most perfect of the world's country-style vegetable dishes.

SNACKS & MAIN COURSE DISHES

Corn Fritters

There is nothing like the taste of fresh corn straight off the cob, but don't despair if this is not readily available. Canned sweetcorn kernels make an ideal substitute.

6   ears of fresh corn or 2 1/2 cups frozen or
     canned corn kernels
3   eggs, well beaten
1/2 cup flour
     Salt
1/2 cup polyunsaturated oil
1/2 cup butter

Cut the corn off the cob in thin slices and collect the kernels in a medium-sized bowl. Blend these or the frozen or canned kernels (drain off liquid) with beaten eggs. Fold in the flour to make a batter that just holds together when dropped into the hot oil. Season with a little salt if desired.

In a deep skillet, heat oil and butter to 375°F. Drop the batter by spoonfuls (tablespoons) into the pan and fry on both sides until golden. It takes about 2 minutes. Remove and dry on paper towels. To keep fritters hot and crunchy, place them on a baking sheet in a warm oven 300°F until ready to serve, but do not keep them in the warming oven for too long lest they lose their crispness. Makes about 30 fritters.

 COOK'S NOTES: To peel tomatoes, drop them into boiling water for a minute, or a little longer in hot sink water, then transfer to cold water to prevent the flesh softening.

Cauliflower Cheese

1 1/2 pounds cauliflower
2   tablespoons butter or margarine
2   tablespoons flour
1/2   cup milk
       Salt and pepper
1/4   teaspoon grated nutmeg
3/4   cup gruyère cheese, grated
2   tablespoons finely chopped parsley
       Sprigs of parsley

Cook the cauliflower whole in plenty of salted boiling water until it just begins to soften; do not overcook. Drain, reserving the cooking water. Break cauliflower into florets, place in an ovenproof dish and keep warm in the oven.

In a saucepan, melt the butter and stir in the flour. Cook gently for 1 minute, then stir in the milk and 1 cup of the reserved cooking water. Bring slowly to a boil, stirring all the time. Lower heat and simmer for 2 minutes, season with salt, pepper and nutmeg. If the mixture is

too thick, add a little more of the cooking water and continue to stir. Add half the cheese and the chopped parsley.

Pour the sauce over the cauliflower, sprinkle the remaining cheese over the top and garnish with parsley sprigs. Serves 4-6.

Pasta with Rocket, Tomatoes & Prosciutto

Rocket has a mustardy taste with a strong bite which is softened by cooking. Its use in this pasta dish is a novel departure from the usual salad approach. Use small spinach leaves if you cannot obtain rocket.

1/2	pound fettucine or linguine
2	tablespoons oil
2	tablespoons butter
1	large garlic clove, chopped
2	thick slices prosciutto, diced
2/3	cup plum tomatoes, peeled and chopped
3	cups rocket, coarsely chopped
	Salt and pepper

Drop pasta into a large pot of boiling salted water to which has been added 1 tablespoon of the oil. Stir until the water returns to a boil, to make sure the pasta strands have not clumped together. Cook for 6 minutes.

At the same time, in a large skillet over a moderate heat, warm half the butter and the remaining oil. Add the garlic and prosciutto and stir for 2 minutes until the garlic is slightly softened but not brown. Set the pan aside.

When the pasta is cooked *al dente*, drain and turn out into a large serving bowl; add the remaining butter and toss.

Return the garlic and prosciutto pan to a high heat until the mixture begins to sizzle. Mix in the tomatoes, then add the rocket, tossing until not quite wilted, about 1 minute. Pour over the pasta in the bowl and season to taste.
Serves 2-3 as a lunch dish.

Tomato Quiche

Although the tomato is a fruit, it has become so much a part of vegetable cuisine that we have no hesitation in including it here. This dish is delicious hot or cold.

FOR THE PASTRY DOUGH (PÂTE BRISÉE)

2	cups flour
5	tablespoons butter
1	egg, lightly beaten
1/2	teaspoon salt
1	tablespoon milk

FOR THE FILLING

8	medium-sized plum tomatoes
2	tablespoons butter
2	large leeks
3	eggs
1/2	cup light cream
2	tablespoons chopped parsley
1	cup thick tomato purée (p. 45)
	Salt and white pepper

Put the flour in a bowl and make a well in the center. Add butter, cut into small pieces, the beaten egg and the salt. Rub all the ingredients together with your fingertips until the mixture resembles bread-crumbs. Mix in the cold milk. Knead the dough until all the ingredients are well mixed. Wrap the dough in plastic wrap and chill in the refrigerator for several hours.

Blanch, peel and halve the tomatoes. Melt half the butter in a large pan and arrange the tomatoes in a single layer. Partially cover the pan and, over a low heat, braise the tomatoes until they are tender but still holding their shape. Wash the leeks and slice into thin rings, extending about 2-inches into the green part. Wash and drain again to remove any dirt or grit. Melt the rest of the butter in a small pan and gently cook the leeks until quite soft.

Served hot or cold, tomato quiche is an eye-catching dish for lunches or light evening meals.

For those who favor the hot, biting flavors of chili and garlic are perfect to mix with spaghetti.

Garlic & Chili Spaghetti

Grease a 10-inch pie plate. Roll out the dough and line the plate with it; press the dough to the sides of the plate and trim off the excess. Set aside while preparing the filling.

In a large mixing bowl, beat the eggs and cream together and stir in the chopped parsley and tomato purée. Season with salt and white pepper. Spoon this mixture into the pie shell. Arrange braised tomato halves around the edge, alternating with a spoonful of the cooked leeks. Make a pattern in the center with any remaining vegetables. Cover the quiche loosely with a sheet of foil and bake in a preheated oven at 375°F for 15 minutes; remove the foil and bake for a further 15 minutes. Serves 4-6.

1	pound spaghetti
1/4	cup oil
5	garlic cloves
5	small red chilies
1/4	cup chopped parsley

Cook the spaghetti *al dente* (until just done) in a large pot containing plenty of salted water and 1 tablespoon of the oil. Chop the garlic and chilies into small pieces and fry in the remaining oil, but do not let the garlic brown as it will taste bitter.

Drain the spaghetti and mix it with garlic-chili oil. Add parsley and serve immediately. Serves 4.

Vegetable Jelly Mold

This is one of those prepare-ahead meals.

1	pound small carrots, thinly sliced
7	ounces scallions
2	pounds asparagus, peeled and cut into 1/4 -inch slices
1 1/2	quarts jelly meat stock (p. 42)
4	sprigs Italian parsley
	Sorrel cream (p. 46)
	or asparagus sauce (p. 43)

Cook the carrots in some boiling salted water for about 8 minutes or until tender but not over-cooked. Remove them from the boiling water and replace them with the scallions. Cook these for 3 minutes and remove. Now add the aspara-gus pieces to the boiling water and cook for 2 to 3 minutes, removing them while they are still bright green. Leave all three vegetables to cool separately.

Take a 3 1/2 pint soufflé dish and pour in a 1/4-inch layer of jelly meat stock. Decorate this with several large parsley leaves. Place in the refrigerator and leave until set. Then add a layer of the carrots followed by the scallions and the asparagus. Pour the remaining cool jelly meat stock over the vegetables and return to the refrigerator until completely set. Unmold onto a flat dish and serve with the sauce of your choice. Serves 8.

Asparagus & Potato Casserole

1	pound cooked asparagus stalks
	Juice of 1 lemon
2	large potatoes, boiled and sliced
	Grated rind of 2 oranges
3	scallions, finely chopped
1	cup fresh bread-crumbs
FOR THE BÉCHAMEL SAUCE	
1	bay leaf
2	slices of onion
6	black peppercorns
4	parsley stalks
2	sprigs of thyme
2	cups milk
1	tablespoon butter
2	tablespoons flour
	Salt and pepper

Marinate the asparagus in the lemon juice for 30 minutes. In a suitable casserole dish, alternate layers of sliced potato and asparagus. Sprinkle each layer with grated orange rind and chopped scallions.

Cover layered vegetables with the béchamel sauce and sprinkle bread-crumbs over. Bake in a preheated oven at 350°F for 30 minutes and serve hot. Serves 4.

TO MAKE BÉCHAMEL SAUCE. Put bay leaf, onion, peppercorns, parsley and thyme in a pan with the milk and gradually bring to a boil over a low heat. Remove and leave to stand. In another saucepan, melt butter and add flour, stirring until the mixture becomes smooth. Remove from the heat and gradually add the strained milk, stirring constantly until thorough-ly blended. Return the saucepan to the heat and stir until the sauce boils and thickens. Season with salt and pepper.

Overleaf: A decorative lattice pie made with gramma squash (p. 40), is a favorite Australian dessert

SALADS

Potato Salad Niçoise

2	pounds small waxy potatoes
1	garlic clove
2	shallots, chopped
3	tablespoons vegetable stock (p. 42)
3	tablespoons dry white wine
2	tablespoons chopped anchovy fillets
1/3	cup oil
1	head of lettuce
2	tablespoons chopped parsley
1	tablespoon chopped basil leaves
1/2	cup black olives
12	cherry tomatoes

Wash and scrub the potatoes. Cover with water and bring to a boil. Simmer for about 20 minutes or until they are just tender but not overdone. Drain and cool slightly. Peel the potatoes while they are still quite warm. Rub the garlic on the inside of a large mixing bowl and place the potatoes in the bowl. Discard the garlic.

Chop the potatoes into largish pieces, about 1-inch cubes, and add the shallots. Pour in the stock and wine, gently mix and set aside until cooled. The potatoes should absorb most of the liquid. Add anchovies and oil and toss so that the potatoes are thoroughly coated.

Arrange the lettuce leaves in a shallow round bowl or on a decorative plate. Turn the potato salad out onto the lettuce leaves, sprinkle with chopped parsley and basil and arrange the olives and tomatoes around the edge. Serves 6-8.

Spinach Salad

1	pound young spinach
1	large Spanish (red) onion
3	hard-cooked eggs
1	cup black olives

FOR THE DRESSING
1/4	cup sour cream
1	medium-size onion, chopped
1	tablespoon red wine vinegar
	Salt and pepper

Wash and dry the spinach. Remove the fibrous stems and center leaf veins. Slice the onion and eggs into rings. Mix all the ingredients together and toss with the dressing. Serves 4.

TO MAKE THE DRESSING. In a blender, combine the sour cream and onion until smooth and set aside in the refrigerator for at least 2 hours. Add the vinegar, then season with the salt and pepper.

Opposite: A salad of finely textured young spinach, decorated with red Spanish onion rings, olives and eggs. Serve with sour cream and vinegar dressing.

 COOK'S NOTES: If using fresh spinach, thoroughly wash it through several changes of cold water to remove all the grit and dirt.

Cucumber & Yogurt Walnut Salad

This dish needs several rests in the preparation time, so you will need to start about 8 hours before the guests arrive. The effort is worthwhile.

3	cucumbers, peeled and scored
	Salt and pepper
	Juice of 4 lemons
1	gelatin, 1/4-ounce envelope
2 1/2	cups yogurt
4	tablespoons chopped walnuts
2	small sweet peppers (1 red, 1 green)

Quarter the cucumbers lengthwise and remove the seed portion. Cut into 1/2-inch pieces and place in a bowl. Season with salt and pepper and pour the lemon juice over. Cover and place in the refrigerator for several hours.

About 4 hours before the salad is required, melt the gelatin in a little warm water and fold gently into the yogurt. Add the cucumber and walnut pieces and place in a decorative bowl. Chill until set.

Before serving, cut the sweet peppers into thin circles, remove seeds and fibrous membranes and decorate the bowl, alternating the colors if possible. Serves 6.

An attractive and healthy salad made from a mixture of freshly picked leaf vegetables, herbs and sweet peppers. The varieties and combinations of vegetables are endless.

White Bean Salad with Sweet Peppers

A colorful and filling salad to serve by itself or as an accompaniment to tuna. You can vary the color of the sweet peppers, if available.

4	cups cooked haricot beans
2	red sweet peppers sliced into thin strips
1	tablespoon chopped chives
8	basil leaves
1	tablespoon chopped marjoram

FOR THE VINAIGRETTE

3	tablespoons oil
2	tablespoons wine vinegar
1	teaspoon superfine sugar
1	teaspoon wholegrain mustard
	Salt

Place the beans in a serving dish and add the sweet peppers. Mix in the herbs, then dress the salad with vinaigrette so that all the beans are well coated. Serves 4-6.

 COOK'S NOTES: To roast sweet peppers, place under a broiler until the skin browns and blisters all over. Remove from heat, cover with a cloth and leave to cool in their own steam.

Baked Onion Salad

An interesting way to prepare onions when all other invention fails you.

7   medium-sized onions, unpeeled
2   tablespoons oil
2   tablespoons rice
1/2 cup water
2/3 cup walnuts, ground
1   teaspoon salt
1   tablespoon wine vinegar

In a preheated oven at 375°F place the onions on a baking sheet and roast them for about 1 1/2 hours or until they are soft and dark brown in color. Allow them to cool, then peel and chop into small pieces.

Heat the oil in a small pan and toss the rice in it for no more than 2 minutes. Add the water, stir, then tightly cover the pan and simmer for 15 minutes or until the rice is soft.

Cool the rice and combine with the onions and walnuts. Dissolve the salt in the vinegar and stir into the rice mixture. Turn out into a serving dish. Serves 4.

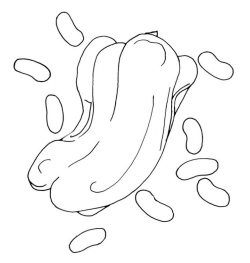

Fresh Garden Salad

Fresh green-leaf vegetables tossed with garden herbs and combined with colorful edible flowers-the best of all salads. You can make as much or as little as you like, so exact quantities really don't come into it; it all depends on how many mouths you have to feed.

Lettuce leaves as available,
iceberg or butter head varieties
Chicory leaves
Young spinach leaves
Sorrel leaves
Rocket leaves
Sprigs of herbs:
basil, mint, parsley, marjoram, chives
Sweet peppers, seeded and cut into rings
Olive oil
Balsamic vinegar

Wash and dry all the salad leaves and herbs thoroughly. In a large bowl or on a big plate, arrange the larger leaves on the bottom and gradually build your salad by overlaying smaller leaves on the top. The herbs are better left as small whole sprigs, interspersed throughout the rest of the vegetables so that you discover little explosions of taste as you munch on through the salad. Decorate the salad with the sweet pepper rings, alternating the colors. Scatter a few nasturtium flowers on top.

You will need no more than a sprinkle of oil and balsamic vinegar over the plate to enhance the natural flavors of the fresh vegetables.

 COOK'S NOTES: The average lemon yields 2 tablespoons of juice.

 COOK'S NOTES: If you want to dull the sharpness of an onion, soak it in cold water for about 20 minutes.

Cooked Celery Salad

1	head celery, leaves and roots removed
1	quart vegetable stock (p. 43)
1/2	cup vinaigrette (p. 47)
1	lettuce, shredded
	Pepper
2	tomatoes, cut into wedges
12	black olives
3	hard-cooked eggs,
	cut into halves or quarters
1	tablespoon anchovy strips

Cut the celery into 6-inch lengths, cover with the stock and cook until just tender, about 10 minutes. Drain and place in a bowl and cover with the vinaigrette. Chill.

Arrange the lettuce on a large serving plate and place the celery around. Season with pepper and garnish the dish with tomato wedges, black olives and egg segments. Drape the anchovy strips over all the ingredients. Drizzle vinaigrette over the salad, if liked. Serves 4.

Broccoli & Cauliflower Salad

A favorite way of eating fresh vegetables in Italy is to cook them *al dente*–that is, just to take the rawness out of them by steaming or boiling, but retaining a crispy-crunchy texture.

3	cups broccoli florets
3	cups cauliflower florets
3	cups mixed stems from both vegetables
1/2	teaspoon salt
1/2	cup vinaigrette (p. 47)

Cut vegetable stems into 2-inch pieces, discarding very thick parts of stalk. Wash the florets and stems then place in boiling water to cover. Add salt and boil for 4-5 minutes, or until just tender. Drain and turn out into a serving dish and pour the vinaigrette over while the vegetables are still warm. This salad may be served either warm or cold. Serves 4.

Asparagus in Vinaigrette

| 2 | pounds asparagus |
| 1/2 | cup vinaigrette (p. 47) |

If the asparagus has very thick ends, peel them before proceeding. Tie the stalks into bundles and boil in salted water for about 7 minutes or until just tender. Drain and remove the ties. Place the asparagus on a serving platter and pour the vinaigrette over while the asparagus is still warm. Serves 4.

Cucumber & Shrimp Salad

One cannot be a purist all the time, so I have sneaked in some shrimp, which offset the greens and combine marvellously with the tangy Vietnamese chili dressing.

2	large cucumbers, peeled and seeded
8	ounces shrimp,
	heads and shells removed
1	cup cress, chopped
2	tablespoons chili dressing (p. 47)
3	tablespoons sesame seeds
1/2	cup mint leaves, chopped

Cut the cucumbers into lengths about the same size as the shrimp. Cut the shrimp in half, lengthwise, and mix with the cucumber pieces and chopped cress. Pour the chili dressing over and stir through.

Brown the sesame seeds in a small, covered, skillet. Do this over a low heat and be careful not to burn the seeds. When you are ready to serve, add the sesame seeds and mint to the salad and toss. Serves 4.

COOK'S NOTES: *If your onions begin to sprout, try using the shoots as a substitute for chives.*

A crunchy salad made from florets of cauliflower and broccoli, chilled and served with vinaigrette dressing.

PRESERVES & SWEETS

WHEN there is a glut of summer vegetables, turning them into relishes or preserving them whole is a marvelous way of keeping these vegetables to enjoy later in the year. Their addition to salad meals is a delightfully delicious finishing touch.

A few basic preparatory steps before you start making your preserves will both save you time and make for a safe environment in the kitchen:

- Think ahead where your preserving jars will be in relation to the hot saucepan; filling those jars is the most difficult and dangerous part of the operation.
- An organized kitchen work surface, kept clear of unnecessary utensils, will get you out of many a jam (pun intended).
- Keep your jars together on a baking sheet while warming them in the oven and later when filling them with the hot preserve. This way, a number of jars are easy to handle in one go, and you also localize any drips or spillage.
- Always use warm jars, as cold ones are likely to crack and render all your hard work useless at the last moment.

 COOK'S NOTES: If recycling instant coffee or jam jars for relishes and preserves, use those with plastic lids, as they are vinegar-proof and will not react with the jar contents as metal lids do.

Eggplant Preserve

Served with green or black olives, this preserve can be eaten as a starter or heated up as an accompaniment to meat dishes.

12	small, long eggplants
6	garlic cloves
1	celery stalk, cut into thin sticks
1/2	cup olive oil
	Salt
3/4	cup spiced herb vinegar
1 1/2	cups refined peanut oil

Wash the eggplants and remove the stalk ends. Slit the vegetables in half lengthwise almost through to their ends. Sandwich small pieces of garlic between two sticks of celery in each eggplant, then fasten the two sides of each eggplant together with toothpicks, previously soaked in water to make them pliable. Pack the eggplants close together in a casserole dish and pour the olive oil over. Cook gently over a medium heat, turning the eggplants over, until they just start to turn brown. Cover the casserole with a lid and simmer for 4 minutes.

Remove the lid, add salt to taste and pour the vinegar over. Continue cooking, turning the eggplants over several times until the cooking liquid evaporates. Remove from the casserole and allow to cool on paper towels. Check that the garlic, celery pieces and toothpicks are in place. Arrange the vegetables in a glass storage jar, making sure they are fully covered by the peanut oil. Seal the jars and store in a cool place.

Eggplant preserve: Long slender eggplants, preserved in a spiced herb vinegar, add a piquant touch to summer salad lunches.

Carrot & Almond Preserve

3   pounds baby carrots, chopped
     Grated rind and juice of 1 lemon or lime
     Granulated sugar, to measure
1   tablespoon chopped blanched almonds
     Rum to measure

Place the carrots in a deep pan and just cover them with water. Simmer until the carrots are quite soft. Drain, then blend in a food processor fitted with the steel blade. Turn out into a large mixing bowl which you have previously weighed. Now weigh the bowl with the purée to find the weight of the purée, and write it

Pickled beans with herbs: preserving vegetables for later use is an old country cooking method. Young, tender French beans bottled in a spicey vinegar are one of my favorites.

down. Add an equal weight of sugar, then mix in the lemon rind and 1 tablespoon of juice.

Simmer the mixture gently over a moderate heat until the preserve thickens. It should come away from the sides of the saucepan. At the last moment stir in the almonds and 1 tablespoon rum for each pound of carrot purée (the weight that you noted down).

Pour preserve into sterilized jars and seal.

34

Corn Relish

1/2	white cabbage
2	large onions
2	small red sweet peppers
5	cups corn kernels, cooked
2	teaspoons salt
2	teaspoons flour
2	teaspoons dry mustard
1/2	teaspoon turmeric
3/4	cup brown sugar
2	cups vinegar

Remove the firm central core from the cabbage and chop the vegetable into small pieces. Chop the onions and sweet peppers, removing seeds,

ribs and any stem parts. Reduce these three vegetables into even smaller pieces by running them through a food processor, fitted with a steel blade, for a few seconds.

In a large cooking pan, combine the corn kernels with the other vegetables, then stir in the spiced vinegar. This is prepared by mixing the salt, flour, mustard, turmeric and sugar together, then gradually stirring in the vinegar until well blended.

Simmer the mixture for 30 minutes, then pack into warm sterilized jars. Cover with melted wax or plastic lids.

Pickled Beans with Herbs

3	cups white wine vinegar
1	small onion, thinly sliced
1	tablespoon granulated sugar
2	tablespoons black peppercorns
2	bay leaves
1/2	teaspoon mace
1	large sprig of thyme or tarragon
1	pound green stringless beans, topped and tailed
1 1/4	quarts water
1	tablespoon salt

Sterilize a preserving jar by boiling and place it in a warm oven to dry. Pour the vinegar into a non-corrosive saucepan and add the onion, sugar, peppercorns, bay leaves, mace and thyme or tarragon. Cover the pan and bring to a boil for 1 minute. Remove from the heat and allow to cool.

In another saucepan, place the beans in the water and add the salt. Bring this to a boil for no more than 2 to 3 minutes, even less if you want a crunchier texture. Drain the beans in a colander and immediately rinse them under cold running water until cool. Pat the beans dry and pack upright in the sterilized jar. Strain the vinegar mixture into the jar to just cover the beans. Seal tightly with a vinegar-proof lid (non-metallic) and store in a cool, dry place for 2 months to mature.

Pickled Onions

I always use the very small pearl or silver skin onions for this recipe. It is very simple, no cooking is involved.and it works well for shallots too. Shallots are very small onions with a mild and delicate flavor. Their outside is red-brown and the flesh has a slight purple tinge. They should not to be confused with scallions, which are sometimes called shallots.

2	pounds pearl pickling onions, skinned
1	tablespoon black peppercorns
1	tablespoon allspice berries
1	tablespoon salt
4	cups brown malt vinegar

Place onions in one large jar or divide them among a number of smaller jars. Using a pestle and mortar, bruise the peppercorns and all-spice, mix with salt and add the mixture to the vinegar. Pour this spiced vinegar over the onions until 1/2-inch of the liquid level is above the onions. Seal with waxed paper or plastic screw tops. Do not use metal lids, as they react with the vinegar. Store for at least a month in a cool, dark place before eating.

Zucchini Relish

3	pounds unpared zucchinis, shredded
3	cups onion, finely chopped
5	tablespoons salt
2 1/2	cups cider vinegar
5	cups sugar
1	tablespoon grated nutmeg
1	tablespoon dry mustard
1	tablespoon turmeric
1	tablespoon cornstarch
1/8	teaspoon cayenne
1	green sweet pepper, chopped
1	red sweet pepper, chopped

Combine the zucchini and onions in a large bowl, sprinkle with the salt and leave to stand overnight. Drain the juices that have collected in the bowl, then rinse the vegetables in cold water and drain once more.

In a large pot combine the zucchini and onion with the rest of the ingredients and bring to a boil, stirring. Reduce the heat and simmer, uncovered, for about 40 minutes until the mixture has reduced and thickened.

Sterilize six jars of 2-cup capacity and spoon the relish into them while hot. Cap and seal tightly.

Vinegars

Flavored vinegars give a real lift to salads and other vegetable dishes but, in view of their acidity, they should be used only in sparing quantities unless otherwise directed. It is always advisable to use a good quality vinegar for your preparations.

Wine and cider vinegars have quite different flavors; brown malt vinegar, because of its caramel coloring agent, will always give a darker color to your pickles, relishes and chutneys than white malt vinegar. Both are of the same strength, so they are interchangeable in recipes-it just depends on your own preferences. Fruit vinegars can, of course, be sweet

and fragrant. The following three recipes are for acidic vinegars which depend for their flavors on readily available, spicey, pungent vegetables. These vinegars can be used in the preparation of vinaigrette (page 47).

Vinegars give zest and variety when sprinkled over salads or combined with oils to make a vinaigrette. Left to right: chili, thyme, shallot, sage. The spiced vinegar preparation is in the foreground.

Garlic Vinegar

2   cups malt vinegar
1   teaspoon chopped garlic

Combine the vinegar and garlic in a glass jar and set aside for 2-3 weeks, shaking occasionally. Strain into bottles and seal.

Rhubarb is often used in pies, desserts and especially in the making of jams, Its somewhat astringent flavor combines well with other vegetables such as carrots, or with sweet fruits like apples and oranges, to make interesting combinations.

Shallot Vinegar

Shallots should not be mistaken for scallions. They are not as strong as either garlic or onions and impart a delicate flavor to the vinegar.

2   cups wine or malt vinegar
2   teaspoons chopped shallot

Put the vinegar in a glass jar and add the shallot. Leave for two weeks, turning the jar every second day. Strain the vinegar into a bottle, seal and label for later use.

Chili Vinegar

1   teaspoon chopped chili
3   small red chilies
2   cups wine vinegar

Place the chopped and whole chilies in a bottle, cover with the vinegar and seal tightly. Leave to marinate for about a month, shaking from time to time.

 COOK'S NOTES: Leeks are often full of mud. Clean them by cutting off the roots, halving the vegetable lengthwise, remove the outer tough coats and separating remaining layers in a sink filled with cold water.

Sweet Potato Dessert

3   pounds red sweet potatoes
1/4   cup packed brown sugar
1/2   cup butter, whipped
2   eggs, beaten
3   tablespoons flour
1/2   cup light cream
1   tablespoon lemon juice
1/2   teaspoon vanilla extract
1/2   cup pecan halves

Boil the sweet potatoes in their jackets until just tender but not too soft. Test by inserting a skewer. Peel and cut the vegetables into small pieces. In a food processor fitted with a metal blade, purée the sweet potatoes, gradually adding the sugar, butter, eggs, flour, cream lemon juice and vanilla.

Grease a shallow ceramic baking dish of 2-quart capacity, or two smaller bowls. Turn the mixture into the dish and top with the pecan halves. Bake for 1 hour in a preheated oven set at 325°F. Serves 8.

Rhubarb & Orange Jam

Even small vegetable gardens usually have at least one large rhubarb plant. Be careful not to eat the leaves, as they are poisonous.

1 1/2   pounds rhubarb, cut into 1-inch lengths
4   large oranges
1   cup water
1 1/2   pounds granulated sugar

Grate the peel from oranges and extract the juice. Scoop out any remaining pulp and set it aside. All you will have left is the pith and the seeds. Chop the pith into small pieces and place in a cheesecloth bag together with the seeds.

In a large bowl, combine rhubarb pieces, orange juice, grated peel, pulp and cheesecloth bag containing seeds and pith. Pour the water over and leave the mixture to rest for 8 hours or overnight.

Transfer the mixture to a large saucepan or preserving pan and bring it to a boil. Lower the heat and simmer for 20 minutes. Remove the cheesecloth bag and add the sugar, stirring until it is fully incorporated. when the setting point is reached (test by seeing if a small amount will jell on a cold saucer), remove from the heat, ladle into sterilized jars and seal.

Gramma Squash Pie

The gramma squash makes wonderful pies. It is a cousin of the pumpkin, which may be substituted if gramma is not available.

FOR THE FILLING

4	cups gramma squash, cooked
	Juice and zest of 2 lemons
1	cup superfine sugar
3/4	cup golden raisins or currants
1/2	teaspoon ground ginger
1/2	teaspoon ground cinnamon
1/2	teaspoon grated nutmeg
2	eggs
1	tablespoon sweet sherry

FOR THE PASTRY DOUGH

2	cups flour
1/2	teaspoon baking powder
1/4	teaspoon salt
2/3	cup butter
1	teaspoon lemon juice
1	egg yolk

In a large mixing bowl, mash the cooked gramma, making sure it has been well drained, or the consistency will be too watery. Add the lemon juice and zest, sugar, dried fruit and spices. Mix well, then beat in the eggs.

Line a 11-inch pie plate with the pastry dough and spoon in the mixture. Decorate the top with 1/2-inch strips of dough to form a lattice pattern and coat with milk or egg yolk, then sprinkle with sugar. Cook in a preheated oven set at 375°F for 35-40 minutes. Serves 8.

TO MAKE THE PASTRY DOUGH

Sift the flour, baking powder and salt, then rub in the butter until the mixture resembles breadcrumbs. Gradually add the lemon juice and egg yolk to form a dry dough. Place on a lightly floured surface and knead into a smooth round ball. Roll out the dough to fit your pie plate, setting a little aside to make the lattice strips.

Pumpkin Cake with Dates

The addition of rich, nourishing dates adds an extra dimension of sweetness to this vegetable-based cake.

1	cup butter
3/4	cup superfine sugar
1	tablespoon grated orange peel
1	teaspoon vanilla extract
2	eggs
1	cup chopped dates
1/2	cup ground almonds
1/2	cup pumpkin, cooked and mashed
2	cups self-rising flour
1/2	cup milk

Cream the butter, sugar, orange rind and vanilla until light and fluffy. Add the eggs one at a time, beating well after each addition. Stir in the dates, almonds and mashed pumpkin; mix well. Add a little of the sifted flour, then some of the milk and stir into the mixture. Continue to do this until all the ingredients have been used. Spread the mixture into a greased, paper-lined 8-inch square cake pan. Bake in a preheated moderate oven 325°F for 1 hour or until cooked when tested with a toothpick.

Carrot Muffins

Muffins, a type of yeasty bread or cake, are delicious served hot for breakfast.

1	cup butter
1	cup superfine sugar
4	eggs
6	cups self-rising flour
1 1/2	cups sour cream
2	cups cooked carrot purée
1/3	cup chopped nuts (optional)

Cream the butter and sugar together until light and fluffy. Beat in the eggs, then add the flour, sour cream and carrot purée. Continue beating until all the ingredients are thoroughly combined. Spoon the mixture into greased 1-cup muffin pans (deep round pans available from kitchenware stores). Sprinkle with nuts, if desired, and bake at 350°F for 25 to 30 minutes or until the muffins turn a golden color.
Makes 20-24 muffins.

Broccoli Muffins

3/4	pound broccoli
1	egg
1	cup milk
2	cups self-rising flour
1/2	teaspoon mixed spice
1	cup rat trap cheese, grated

Break the broccoli into small florets and wash thoroughly. Whisk the egg and milk together in a mixing bowl, then sift in the flour and mixed spice. Stir until the mixture is just combined. Finally, fold in the broccoli and grated cheese. Spoon the mixture into lightly greased 1-cup muffin pans. Bake in a preheated moderately hot oven 375°F for 30 minutes.
Makes 10 muffins.

Carrot & Walnut Cake

Carrots are rich in vitamins A, B and C and, because of their very pleasant flavor, they are used frequently in sweet and savory dishes, especially in cakes where they add moistness and a lightness to the texture. Use young, fresh carrots wherever possible.

2	eggs
1	cup superfine sugar
3/4	cup vegetable oil
1/2	teaspoon vanilla extract
1	teaspoon bicarbonate of soda
1	cup flour
1/2	teaspoon mixed spice
1/2	teaspoon salt
1 1/2	cups carrot, finely grated
1/2	cup walnuts, chopped
FOR THE CREAM CHEESE FROSTING	
2	tablespoons butter whipped
1/4	cup cream cheese
1	teaspoon grated lemon peel
1 1/2	cups confectioner sugar

Combine all the cake ingredients, except for the carrots and walnuts, in a large mixing bowl. Stir with a wooden spoon until the mixture is smooth, or beat on low speed in a food processing machine. Stir in the carrot and walnuts. Pour the mixture into an 8-inch ring tin which has been well greased. Bake in a preheated moderate oven 325°F for 45 minutes. When cooked, leave the cake to stand for 5 minutes before turning out to cool on a wire rack.

Beat the whipped butter and cream cheese together until the mixture is smooth and creamy. Add the lemon peel and sifted confectioner sugar and continue beating until the frosting is quite smooth. Ice the cake with a spatula.

Pumpkin Biscuits

2   tablespoons butter
2   tablespoons superfine sugar
1/2   cup pumpkin, cooked and mashed
1   egg
1/2   cup milk
2 1/2 cups self-rising flour

Cream the butter and sugar until light and fluffy. Add the mashed pumpkin and egg and beat thoroughly. Slowly add the milk and sifted flour, mixing all the time. Turn the dough out onto a floured board and knead lightly. Roll out the dough until about 1-inch thick. Cut into rounds and place on a floured baking sheet. Cook in a preheated hot oven 425°F for 20 minutes or until cooked through when tested. Turn out on a wire rack to cool.

Caramel Cornflake Cookies

Tasty biscuits made from breakfast cereal.

1/2   cup butter
1/2   cup dark brown sugar
1/2   cup superfine sugar
1/2   cup dry coconut
3   cups cornflakes
1/2   cup nuts, finely chopped
1   egg

Melt the butter over low heat, add the sugars and stir until the mixture is well combined. Add the coconut, lightly crushed cornflakes, nuts and beaten egg. Mix well. Place teaspoonfuls of the mixture on greased baking sheets, firming each cookie with fingers. Bake in a preheated moderate oven 350°F for 10 minutes or until golden-brown. Leave on the baking sheet for about 5 minutes, then transfer to a wire rack to cool. Makes about 30 cookies.

STOCKS & SAUCES

Jelly Meat Stock

If you want to keep this stock for some time, store it in the freezer. If kept in the refrigerator, then boil it up every few days to prevent spoilage. A tasty jelly stock is essential when making molds or mousses.

1/2   pound pork rind
2   calf's feet
1   veal knuckle
1/2   pound chicken wings
3   quarts water
       Salt
2   onions
8   whole cloves
2   carrots, peeled
1   whole garlic head
       A bouquet garni
2   celery stalks, cut into quarters

Wash clean the pork rind and calf's feet by boiling together for no more than 5 minutes, draining then rinse under cold water. Place all the meat on a wire rack in a large stockpot and cover with water. Slowly bring to a boil, continually taking off the scum that rises to the surface. Season with salt and add the rest of the ingredients, sticking the cloves into one of the onions. Cover the pot, adjusting the lid so that the steam can escape. Reduce the heat to a very low level and simmer for 5 hours.

Dampen a piece of cheesecloth with warm water and wring it out. Line a strainer with cheesecloth and strain the stock into a large bowl. Cool and refrigerate the stock until it has set. Skim off the fat which rises to the top; all of the fat must be removed for a clean jelly stock.

Basic Chicken Stock

If you buy commercially prepared products, you are generally getting little more than salt. Fresh stock is easy and inexpensive to make and can be stored in containers in the refrigerator or in the freezer as small frozen blocks.

3   pounds chicken carcasses
4   celery stalks, coarsely chopped
3 1/2 quarts cold water
6   carrots, unpeeled, thickly sliced
2   brown onions, quartered
8   black peppercorns

Put the chicken pieces in a large pan and rinse with hot water. Drain and add the cold water along with the other ingredients. Bring to a boil, then simmer for 2 hours. Skim off and discard the scum that forms when the pot begins to simmer. The stock will be rather tasteless as it has no salt; this is added when you use the stock in the preparation of soups and other dishes.

Basic Vegetable Stock

10   medium-sized carrots
5   medium-sized onions
      Half a head of celery, including leaves
1   tablespoon butter
4-5   black peppercorns
1   teaspoon tomato paste
      Vegetable scraps

Chop the vegetables and brown them in butter in a large saucepan. Add all the other ingredients and cover with water. Bring to a boil, cover and simmer for 2 hours. Strain the liquid and cool. The stock will keep in the refrigerator for a few days, or freeze it in ice-cube trays.

Asparagus Sauce

Asparagus sauce can be used to add flavor to cold vegetable dishes.

1   tablespoon margarine
1   tablespoon flour
1 1/2 cups fresh or canned asparagus stalks,
      drained and liquid reserved
3   tablespoons light cream
      Salt and pepper

Melt the margarine in a saucepan and sprinkle the flour over it. Stir over low heat for a few minutes. Gradually add the asparagus liquid to the pan, stirring all the time, until the mixture is thick and smooth.

Remove from the heat and stir in the cream. In a food processor, blend the asparagus stalks to a smooth purée and pour into the cream mixture. Season to taste with pepper and salt and return the saucepan to the heat. Stir gently till heated through. Makes 1-cup of sauce.

Thick Tomato Purée

This purée can be used as the basis of other sauces, or as a garnish, or to fill mushrooms and other vegetables.

3	*pounds ripe tomatoes*
1	*tablespoon oil*
2	*shallots, chopped*
1	*bay leaf*
6	*basil leaves*
	Salt and pepper

Blanch the tomatoes for 5 minutes in very hot water. Peel and core them and chop into small pieces. Heat the oil and butter in a large pan, add the shallots and sauté until golden.

Add the tomatoes and the herbs and cook over a low heat, stirring frequently, until the tomatoes are soft. Discard the bay leaf, then transfer the mixture to a food processor and blend.

Return the purée to the pan and simmer until the mixture has reduced and reached a thick consistency. Season with salt and pepper. Makes about 3 cups.

Vegetable stocks add real body to your dishes. Use fresh or left over vegetable pieces.

Sorrel Cream Sauce

Sorrel cream sauce is a quickly made, delicious sauce to accompany other vegetable dishes.

A simply made, tart sauce for beans, asparagus, summer squash, cauliflower and other not too strongly flavored vegetables.

6   *cups sorrel leaves, washed*
1/3   *cup light cream*
1/8   *teaspoon salt*

Cut the sorrel leaves into thin strips and combine with the cream in a small, non-aluminum saucepan. Bring to a boil and simmer, mashing the leaves until incorporated with the cream. This should take 4 minutes. Season with the salt. Makes about 3/4 cup.

Chili Dressing, Vietnamese-Style

If you follow this recipe, you will have enough dressing for at least two meals. It's always easy to double or triple the quantities if you want more. A good thing about it is its long life. It will keep in the refrigerator for several months as long as the container is kept tightly closed. Nuoc mam is a fermented fish sauce available from most Oriental food stores.

2	small red chilies, chopped and seeded
1	garlic clove, chopped
1	teaspoon superfine sugar
	Pulp of half a lime
1	tablespoon vinegar
1	tablespoon water
4	tablespoons nuoc mam

Using a pestle and mortar, crush the chilies and garlic with the sugar. Add lime pulp and continue to blend. Mix the pulp with the rest of the ingredients; if you want a more cohesive mixture, transfer the mixture to a food processor fitted with a steel blade and blend.

Vinaigrette

Vinaigrette is the French word for little vinegar and is a salad dressing made with oil, vinegar and seasonings. You may wish to change the proportions from time to time, depending on the tartness and flavor of vegetable you are going to dress, or because of the strength and flavor of the vinegar you are going to use.

1	teaspoon salt
1/4	teaspoon pepper
2	tablespoons wine vinegar
1/2	cup oil

Combine the salt and pepper in a small bowl and add the vinegar. Stir until the salt is dissolved. Pour in the oil, stirring or beating with a small whisk until the oil is incorporated. Makes 1/2 cup.

Different flavors can be obtained by substituting spicey vegetable vinegars (p. 38-39) for wine vinegar. Other variations include:

GREEN VINAIGRETTE: Just before you add the oil, stir in 2 tablespoons of chopped spinach which has been squeezed dry, 1 tablespoon of fines herbes and 1 tablespoon of chopped cress. Blend in a food processor.

TOMATO VINAIGRETTE: Add 2 tablespoons of thick tomato purée (p. 45) to the prepared vinaigrette.

FRESH HERB VINAIGRETTE: Add 1 tablespoon of chopped mixed herbs, such as basil, mint and marjoram, or use the herbs individually.

CURRY VINAIGRETTE: To your basic vinaigrette add 1 tablespoon of chopped onion which has previously been cooked with 1 teaspoon of curry powder and 1 crushed garlic clove in 1 teaspoon of oil. Blend the mixture with the vinaigrette in a food processor.

INDEX

Page numbers in **bold** type indicate illustrations.